DATE DUE

MAY 1 7 1977			
SEP 1 9 1979			
30 505 JOSTEN'S			

JAMES
WELDON
JOHNSON

JAMES WELDON JOHNSON

By **OPHELIA SETTLE EGYPT**

illustrated by **MONETA BARNETT**

THOMAS Y. CROWELL COMPANY • **NEW YORK**

CROWELL BIOGRAPHIES
Edited by Susan Bartlett Weber

JANE ADDAMS *by Gail Faithfull Keller*

MARIAN ANDERSON *by Tobi Tobias*

LEONARD BERNSTEIN *by Molly Cone*

MARTHA BERRY *by Mary Kay Phelan*

WILT CHAMBERLAIN *by Kenneth Rudeen*

RAY CHARLES *by Sharon Bell Mathis*

CESAR CHAVEZ *by Ruth Franchere*

SAMUEL CLEMENS
by Charles Michael Daugherty

ROBERTO CLEMENTE *by Kenneth Rudeen*

CHARLES DREW *by Roland Bertol*

FANNIE LOU HAMER *by June Jordan*

LANGSTON HUGHES, AMERICAN POET
by Alice Walker

JAMES WELDON JOHNSON
by Ophelia Settle Egypt

FIORELLO LA GUARDIA
by Mervyn Kaufman

THE MAYO BROTHERS *by Jane Goodsell*

JOHN MUIR *by Charles P. Graves*

JESSE OWENS *by Mervyn Kaufman*

GORDON PARKS *by Midge Turk*

ROSA PARKS *by Eloise Greenfield*

THE RINGLING BROTHERS *by Molly Cone*

JACKIE ROBINSON *by Kenneth Rudeen*

ELEANOR ROOSEVELT *by Jane Goodsell*

MARIA TALLCHIEF *by Tobi Tobias*

JIM THORPE *by Thomas Fall*

THE WRIGHT BROTHERS
by Ruth Franchere

MALCOLM X *by Arnold Adoff*

Library of Congress Cataloging in Publication Data Egypt, Ophelia Settle. James Weldon Johnson. (A Crowell biography) SUMMARY: Brief biography of the turn-of-the-century black author, educator, lawyer, and diplomat who started the first Negro daily newspaper in the United States. 1. Johnson, James Weldon, 1871-1938—Juv. lit. [1. Johnson, James Weldon, 1871-1938. 2. Authors, American. 3. Negroes—Biography] I. Barnett, Moneta, illus. II. Title. PS3519.02625Z65 818'.5'209 [B] [92] 73-9521 ISBN 0-690-00214-9 ISBN 0-690-00215-7 (lib. bdg.)

2   3   4   5   6   7   8   9   10

A CROWELL
BIOGRAPHY

"Hey, Jim! What's it going to sound like if we play it on the black keys?"

A slow smile spread over James Weldon Johnson's face and made tiny crinkles around his bright gray eyes. He looked down at his six-year-old brother, Rosamond, seated beside him on the piano bench. Rosamond loved music. Making up funny songs on the piano was his favorite game.

"Let's play it and see," James answered. His thin fingers touched the keys.

"You play it on the black keys up there, and I'll play it on the white keys down here."

Noisy tinkles and rumbles, mixed with the sound of the boys' voices, filled the room and drifted out to the porch of the white house with the green shutters. James and Helen Johnson sat there listening to their young sons.

"I wish they'd use the right names for those keys and stop saying the white keys and the black keys," James heard his mother say.

He enjoyed hearing people talk. He liked words and the way people used them. He loved words as much as his brother loved music.

James hit the keys very lightly, so that he could listen.

"I never worry about Rosamond," his fa-

2

ther said. "He loves music. He'll make his living that way. But I do worry about Jim."

James sat very still.

His father kept talking. "I wonder if Jim will ever settle down to one job. He likes to do so many different things."

"I don't think we need to worry," said Mrs. Johnson gently. "Whatever he does, he does well. He will be all right."

Suddenly James did not feel like playing the piano any longer. He wanted to be alone, so

3

he could think. He slid off the piano bench and tiptoed through the house to the back yard.

Eight-year-old James knew that what his father said was true. He did like to do many things. Still he didn't want his father to worry. He loved his father very much.

Mr. Johnson had not had a chance to go to school, but he had taught himself to read and write English and Spanish. He taught his sons to speak Spanish. James liked the strange new words.

James thought of the stories his mother had read to him when he was younger. The words from the stories always seemed to spin James away from his small bed. He felt as if everything happening in the stories was happening to him. He especially liked the stories about Black people. Such stories made him feel proud. Many times he fell asleep making up stories of his own.

But that night James Weldon Johnson fell asleep hoping that he would learn to do one thing well. While he slept, moonlight danced on the dark green leaves of the orange tree outside his window. The neighborhood was quiet.

Nobody knew that the tired, long-legged boy who had just climbed into bed would grow up to be a writer, or that he would be known all over the world because of his songs and poems and books. Nobody in the neighborhood knew that the pride that James Weldon Johnson felt for his people would one day burst forth in stirring words that would lift the hearts of Black people everywhere.

James Weldon Johnson was born June 17, 1871, in an old weather-beaten house in Jack-

sonville, Florida. He was still a baby when his father built a new house.

Building the house was not easy, especially after Mr. Johnson had worked long hours on his job in the St. James Hotel dining room. Often he felt too tired to work on the house. But when he thought of his family, he forgot his tiredness and kept building.

Mr. Johnson spent his days off with his boys. He took them for long walks. They splashed around in the river together. He taught them how to swim and how to fly a kite.

Most of all, James enjoyed their talks. He liked to tell about the things he saw. His father always listened.

James' love for words made him the best student in his English class at Stanton Elementary School. He loved the books he found

there. People in books seemed real to him.

James wrote his first story at Stanton. He didn't know it then, but he had started his first career.

Even while he was working, James found a way to enjoy words. While he was in school, he got up at four o'clock every morning to deliver newspapers. Before he made his last delivery, he read the whole paper.

James also liked to play baseball. He was the best pitcher in his Florida league. "Baseball was my game," he said. "I had a lot of tricky pitches, like my wide-out curve ball. I practiced every day with my catcher."

Once James and his catcher were invited to
play with a men's team. People started laughing at the small pitcher in his league uniform.
But they soon stopped laughing. James struck
out sixteen men. His team won the game.

When James finished the eighth grade and
was ready for high school, there was no place
for him to go. The high school in Jacksonville
was for white children only. His father and
mother finally decided to send him to Atlanta,
Georgia. There he would attend the high
school at Atlanta University, a school for
Blacks, where students were prepared for
college.

James ran to tell his brother. "Hey, Rozy!"
he yelled. "I'm going to Atlanta University!"

Instead of returning James' smile, Rosamond stared sadly at his brother.

James' smile faded. Slowly it dawned on him that he would be leaving his brother, his father and mother, and all his friends.

Mr. Johnson had a different worry. He was afraid James might have trouble on the train. Some conductors tried to make every Black person ride in the baggage car.

Mr. Johnson had always refused to go there. Once James had been with his father when the conductor ordered him to move.

"I'm an American citizen," Mr. Johnson said. "I'll sit where I please." James, his eyes filled with pride, snuggled close to his father.

"Don't let these conductors scare you, son," his father had said. "Always stand up for your rights."

Waiting for the train to take him to Atlanta, James did not think of trouble. He was busy saying good-bye to his friends. He blinked back his tears when he kissed his mother,

and followed his father to a seat on the train.

"No matter what happens," Mr. Johnson said before he left his son, "don't give up your seat."

Soon the conductor came around to collect the tickets. He spoke gruffly to James. "You'd better get out of this car and into the one ahead."

James felt scared, but he was angry, too. "I have a first-class ticket," he said. "This is the first-class car, isn't it?"

The conductor tried to make him move. But James stayed where he was. Finally the conductor left him alone.

The next day the puffing engine pulled the train into Atlanta.

Right away James liked Atlanta University with its ivy-covered, red brick buildings, its green lawns, and tall trees. He liked his studies, too, and did well in them. He became captain of the baseball team. He wrote poems that were printed in the school newspaper. Soon everybody in the school knew who James Weldon Johnson was.

Still, James wanted to do more.

He kept remembering something that had happened when he was a little boy. His mother had taught him to recite a poem for a

Sunday school program. He had practiced it over and over without making a mistake. But when it was time for him to speak, he couldn't remember a single word. He had run off the stage in tears.

"It's all right, James Weldon," his mother had said. "You'll do better next time."

Next time is now, James thought. He joined a club where students learned to speak in public. Soon it was his turn to take part in a speaking contest. He wrote his speech and practiced it every night.

On the night of the contest the school auditorium was filled with students and teachers. James walked slowly across the stage. He could not stop his hands and knees from shaking. But he managed to begin. Slowly his nervousness left him. When he finished his speech, the people clapped loudly.

After that night James was no longer afraid to speak to crowds.

At the end of his first year in college James found a summer job as a teacher. His school was in a country church in Georgia. The children had to walk many miles to get there. They sat on hard, scratchy, wooden benches and used their laps for desks.

Often James told them stories of great Black leaders, like Frederick Douglass, a slave who escaped to the North and led the fight to free other slaves. James also wrote funny poems that made the children laugh. They loved their warm, friendly teacher. He made them feel good inside and proud to be Black.

James did not want to leave when summer ended. He liked these children and their parents. He liked their preacher's sermons, too. The words the preacher used and the way he said them made his melodious sermons sound like poems. James tucked the idea of writing a book of sermons away in his mind with his other memories of that summer.

James Weldon did not get back to his country school. But that was not the end of his teaching.

After he was graduated from college, he became principal of Stanton Elementary School in Jacksonville. Only a few years before, he had been a student there.

There was still no high school for Black children. So James started a ninth grade at Stanton and taught most of the classes himself. He kept adding teachers and classes until Stanton became a high school with all twelve grades.

James still found time to write poems. He was jubilant when he sold one of his poems to a famous magazine. His brother, Rosamond,

was graduated from a Boston music school and
came home full of ideas for songs and plays.
He asked James to help him write them.

21

From then on, the two brothers spent their summers in New York City. With a friend, Bob Cole, they wrote about people working, playing, singing, and falling in love. Their songs and musical plays were printed and sold. Many were big hits.

Each fall James and Rosamond returned to their home in Jacksonville. Sometimes they wrote songs for the Stanton schoolchildren and other groups in town. Their most famous song was written for a celebration of Abraham Lincoln's birthday.

Lincoln was President of the United States during the Civil War. To help end the war, he freed most of the slaves. So every year Black people in Jacksonville had a program to honor his memory. This year James was going to make a speech.

"I have my speech ready," James said to his brother as they sat together on the porch one night. "But I want to do something else, too."

"Like what?" Rosamond asked.

James thought for a moment. "Maybe a song about slavery and freedom," he answered.

"That's it!" Rosamond said. "Something children can sing."

Rosamond went inside and sat down at the piano. His fingers began to move over the keys.

James walked back and forth on the porch. He was trying to bring the words from deep within him. Finally the first words came. "Lift every voice and sing," he began, speaking the words aloud.

He thought of the dark past of slavery and of the hope that emancipation had brought. He thought of the real freedom that Black people still could not claim. Slowly the words began to flow. James sat down, wrote the first stanza, and passed it to Rosamond inside.

Soon the words came so fast James' fingers seemed to fly over the paper. They could not keep up with the rush of words in his head. Tears of joy streamed down his cheeks.

24

When he finished the last line, he sat listening while Rosamond composed the music to match the words.

On the day of the celebration there was not a single empty seat in the huge auditorium. In front sat five hundred schoolchildren. They listened quietly to their principal's speech.

"We have a surprise for you," James said next. "A new song, called 'Lift Every Voice and Sing.'"

Soon the stirring words and music filled the hall. When the last stanza ended, everyone was standing. For a long moment they stood very, very still. Then their cheers filled the hall. They knew that "Lift Every Voice and Sing" was their song.

The summer after the celebration Rosamond moved to New York. Every year when school closed James went to join him. They stayed at a hotel. There, with Bob Cole, they kept writing songs and plays.

"Why don't you stay in New York?" Rosamond asked James. "We need you here all the time."

"I keep thinking of the children at Stanton," James answered. "Besides, I don't know whether I can earn enough money to live on without my job."

Finally he wrote the school superintendent in Jacksonville that he would not return. When he dropped the letter in the mailbox, he felt that he had made the right decision.

James Weldon Johnson did make a good living. Sometimes he earned more in a week than he had in a whole year at Stanton. He also wrote his first book. It was a story about the problems Black people face in America.

Although James Weldon Johnson did many different things, he did not work all the time. He enjoyed concerts, parties, and plays. At a

party in New York, he met a beautiful girl
named Grace Nail. They were married in
1910.

Later, they went to visit James' mother in
Jacksonville. James ran up the steps of his old
home and hugged his mother. Laughing, he
swung her off her feet and whirled her around
and around.

"Put me down this minute, James Weldon!" she said. Her face was full of laughter,
but her eyes were bright with tears. She lived

29

alone now. Mr. Johnson had died the year
before.

Over the years James and Grace visited
Mrs. Johnson often. Sometimes Rosamond
went with them.

James was invited to many places to speak

and to read from his writings. One night he sat in a crowded church, waiting his turn to talk. He was tired after a busy day, and blinked his eyes to keep from falling asleep.

"Once upon a time," the tall Black preacher was saying, "there was no world. Nothing but darkness everywhere." He paced back and forth in the pulpit and boomed out the words of his story.

James remembered the moving sermons he had heard a long time ago in Georgia, and his tiredness melted away.

"No land, no water, no people, no birds"—the preacher's deep musical voice filled the church—"Not even one little star. Then God stepped out of his heaven and hurled the earth into space!"

The people began shouting and humming, keeping time with the preacher's rhythm. Before the sermon ended, James had started

writing a poem. He called it "The Creation."
It began:

And God stepped out on space,
And he looked around and said:
I'm lonely—
I'll make me a world. . . .

At first it was black dark.

Then God smiled,
And the light broke,

And the darkness rolled up on one side,
And the light stood shining on the other. . . .
Then God reached out and took the light in his
    hands,

And God rolled the light around in his hands
Until he made the sun;
And he set the sun a-blazing in the heavens. . . .

Later "The Creation" and other sermon-poems were printed in a book called *God's Trombones.* These poems were also made into a play.

James Weldon Johnson wrote many other books. With his brother he collected and published two books of Negro spirituals. James did not want people to forget those songs Black slaves had made up and sung. Many spirituals like "Deep River" and "Go Down Moses" show the slaves' longing for freedom.

While James was writing, he had a full-time job with the national office of the NAACP in New York. The NAACP is an organization of men and women who believe that Black people should have the same rights as other Americans.

One of James Weldon Johnson's toughest fights for the NAACP was against lynchings. Often a Black person accused of a crime never got a chance to be tried in court. A gang of white people would drag him into the woods and hang him, or tie him to a tree and burn him to death. This kind of murder is called lynching. Sometimes a Black man was lynched for talking back to a white person.

Almost one hundred Black people were lynched in 1919. That year James started his fight to get the United States government to pass a law to stop lynching. Although he fought hard, the law was not passed. Still, so

much talk about the horror of lynching fright-
ened people. They found ways to stop most of
these mob murders.

When James Weldon Johnson was almost
sixty years old, he decided to teach in the

South again. This time
he went to Fisk University
in Nashville, Tennessee.
There he taught students
to write stories, plays,
poems, and songs.

"A proud light shines in his eyes," the
students said, "when he reads from books
Black people have written. . . ."

His students felt happy working with him. They learned to write with pride about Black people.

James liked the quiet peaceful life at Fisk. There he finished writing the story of his life, *Along This Way.*

Many people did not know that while he was still in Jacksonville, James Weldon Johnson published a daily newspaper. They did not know that he also became a lawyer, or that for seven years he was United States consul in Venezuela and Nicaragua. *Along This Way* described these experiences, and many others. It told of James Weldon Johnson's dreams to keep on teaching and writing.

In the summer of 1938, James and his wife went to Maine on vacation. One day when they were out driving, their car was hit by a train. His wife was badly hurt. James Weldon Johnson was killed.

Today, this gentle, wise, creative man, who worked so hard to help his people, seems very much alive. He lives in his songs, his poems, and his books. He lives through the work of the students he taught. He lives in the work he did to win equal rights for Black people.

When Blacks stand to sing their national

song, "Lift Every Voice and Sing," its words speak to them in a very special way. When they sing of the dark days of slavery, they feel sad. When they sing of the long way Blacks have come since emancipation, they feel proud. When they sing of the hard fight for freedom they still must win, they feel strong, and ready to "march on till victory is won."

LIFT EVERY VOICE AND SING*

Lift every voice and sing,
Till earth and heaven ring,
Ring with the harmonies of liberty;
Let our rejoicing rise
High as the listening skies,
Let it resound loud as the rolling sea.

Sing a song full of the faith that the dark
    past has taught us;
Sing a song full of the hope that the present
    has brought us;
Facing the rising sun of our new day begun,
Let us march on till victory is won.

Stony the road we trod,
Bitter the chast'ning rod,
Felt in the days when hope unborn had died;
Yet with a steady beat,
Have not our weary feet
Come to the place for which our fathers sighed?
We have come over a way that with tears has been
    watered;
We have come, treading our path through the blood
    of the slaughtered,
Out of the gloomy past,
Till now we stand at last
Where the white gleam of our bright star is cast.

God of our weary years
God of our silent tears,
Thou who hast brought us thus far on our way;
Thou who hast by Thy might,
Led us into the light,
Keep us forever in the path, we pray.
Lest our feet stray from the places, our God, where
  we met Thee,
Lest, our hearts drunk with the wine of the world,
  we forget Thee;
Shadowed beneath Thy hand,
May we forever stand
True to our God,
True to our native land.

ABOUT THE AUTHOR

Ophelia Settle Egypt's admiration and affection for James Weldon Johnson go back to her early childhood and "the joyous pride with which we sang 'Lift Every Voice and Sing.'" Then there were the Cole-Johnson Broadway hits so popular during her college days. And in the late twenties and early thirties, Mrs. Egypt was a young instructor at Fisk University when Johnson was there as the first Professor of Creative Literature, and she was "his most ardent fan."

Born in Clarksville, Texas, Mrs. Egypt spent her childhood there and in Langston, Oklahoma, and her high school years in Denver, Colorado. She holds degrees from Howard University, the University of Pennsylvania, and the New York School of Social Work. In 1970 she retired with many honors from a long and intensively varied career in social work, and she is now concentrating on writing. JAMES WELDON JOHNSON is her first book, although she has had many articles published. She lives in Washington, D.C., where she is an active member of the Black Writers Workshop, and she spends much time with a five-year-old grandson and an infant granddaughter.

ABOUT THE ARTIST

Moneta Barnett lives and works in Brooklyn, where she was born. She studied art at the Brooklyn Museum Art School and at Cooper Union. Her illustrations for JAMES WELDON JOHNSON reflect her deep interest in "the historical and cultural role of Afro-Americans in America."